BE NICE and WIN ™

Jonathan S. Blank

Chad Publishing

Published by Chad Publishing, Inc.
11330 Lakefield Drive
Building II, Suite 200
Duluth, GA 30097
770.814.4140
www.beniceandwin.com

Manufactured in the United States of America

Library of Congress Control Number: 2006903524

ISBN 0-9779835-0-1
Printed in Canada

Cover and book design by Jill Dible

INTRODUCTION

Professors at Harvard Business School and Duke University's Fuqua School of Business came to some interesting conclusions in their recently published study:

1. Being "nice" at work is a great asset;
2. Nice employees have hidden value to a business, and to themselves;
3. Businesses would profit from "identifying and protecting" their nice employees; and
4. Businesses would profit from "strategically positioning" their nice employees so they can spread their value across the entire business. (*Harvard Business Review*, June 2005, available at www.beniceandwin.com)

Be Nice and Win: How Nice People Succeed in Business is the first book I know of that is dedicated entirely to helping nice people win at business, and helping businesses win through their nice people. It puts the Harvard/Duke study into practice with time-proven consensus expert advice that builds on the strengths of nice people, simplified into three easy and effective Strategies for Success in a fun and quick-reading "business fable" format.

In doing so, *Be Nice and Win* delivers two important messages for individual readers and for businesses on behalf of their customers and employees.

First, it says "yes, nice people can *and should* win at work." It shows us that the experts' consensus advice – the advice they agree on – is perfectly suited to helping nice people succeed in business. This hits home for all nice people who have ever wondered whether they are really too nice to succeed in business.

In addition, *Be Nice and Win* delivers an important ethics message: even in today's competitive business world, you can still be nice – and win; that people are still best served by taking the high-road to success because "it's the nice thing to do, it's the right thing to do, and it's the way to succeed."

As an executive with seventeen years in client-service professions, I know how busy people feel – endlessly pressed for time and on the move. I wanted to make *Be Nice and Win* as easy and effective as possible for them, in form and in substance. That is why I was delighted when one of my proofreaders noted that *Be Nice and Win* is "an ideal book for the train, plane, beach or bedside," a fun and fast read that you can finish in just a few hours.

As someone who heads his own business, I am also keenly aware of how important it is for businesses to ensure that their people work together with optimal productivity. I wanted *Be Nice and Win* to be a welcome resource to help their employees enhance their people skills, teamwork skills, and work-quality skills.

Just as businesses use *Who Moved My Cheese?* to help employees deal with change, it is my hope that businesses will use *Be Nice and Win* to help employees – be nice and win.

Helping businesses win, and helping people to *Be Nice and Win*. That is what my work is all about.

Jonathan Blank
Atlanta, Georgia

BE NICE and WIN™

*"The most important single ingredient in the formula
of success is knowing how to get along with people."*
— PRESIDENT THEODORE ROOSEVELT

Once upon a time there was a Nice Man. The Nice Man was a very typical man. He was bright, had a good family and worked hard at his job.

He was quite content.

But as time passed the Nice Man became less content. He was not making as much money as he wanted – as much money as he needed. Nor was he getting the promotions he thought he deserved.

One evening after work the Nice Man was in a particularly not-nice mood.

"I just don't believe it," he said as he entered the front door, coat and briefcase in his arms.

"You don't believe what?" asked his wife as she met him in the center of the room with a kiss.

The Nice Man sulked over to his chair, put down his coat and briefcase and began to explain. "I didn't get the promotion that I applied for. They took someone else from my department. So now I'm stuck in the same position, same salary, same boring work for yet another year!"

"Oh, I'm so sorry to hear that," consoled his wife.

"I just don't understand why I'm not moving up faster, why I can't get the promotion and raise that I want so badly, that *we need* so badly."

He looked up sadly at his wife and said, "You know what my problem is?"

"What?" asked his wife.

"My problem is that I'm too nice. I'm too nice to succeed in business. I'm too nice to my colleagues, I'm too nice to my boss, I'm too nice to everyone. Nice people finish last in business, and being nice is what's holding me back."

"Oh, I'm sure that's not true," his wife said, trying to be sympathetic.

"Oh, it's true. But the thing is, I just can't turn myself into a nasty you-know-what. I just don't have it in me."

"I know you don't," his wife said, "and that's why I love you and married you. I love you for who you are – a nice man. And I'm sure being a nice man is not what's holding you back at work."

"Well," said the Nice Man, "it certainly seems that way."

"Perhaps," said his wife, looking for some resolution, "this is something you might want to talk about with Uncle Prius. After all, he built one of the largest businesses in the state and he is also one of the nicest people I have ever met. He has so many friends, you can't even count them. The only thing he has more of than friends is money! Everyone likes Uncle Prius, and he has gone from rags to riches even while being nice."

"Well," said the Nice Man, "I don't want to trouble Uncle Prius with my problems, but I agree with what you're saying. Uncle Prius is very successful, runs a huge conglomerate that he built from scratch, and everyone certainly does like him."

"Go ahead," said his wife. "Give Uncle Prius a call. Ask him what he thinks."

"Okay," said the Nice Man. "I will."

And the Nice Man called Uncle Prius, who was only too happy to have him over to his office the very next day.

"Come in, son, come in," Uncle Prius said. "So glad to see you," he added, taking the Nice Man's hand in a firm shake.

"Thank you, Uncle Prius. I greatly appreciate you taking time from your busy day to speak with me."

"Don't be ridiculous," Uncle Prius responded as he and the Nice Man sat down around a small coffee table in Uncle Prius' office. "It's my pleasure to help out any way I can. You mentioned on the phone that you wanted to talk about your work."

"Yes," said the Nice Man, looking a bit depressed. "Things are not going exactly the way I'd like."

"Do you need money, my boy? Because if you do, then just ask!"

"No, no, not at all," the Nice Man insisted. "I'm paying my bills just fine, even have a bit of savings."

"That's quite commendable," said Uncle Prius. "So what's on your mind?"

"Well, if I can speak openly with you . . ."

"No other way," Uncle Prius insisted.

The Nice Man looked up at Uncle Prius and said, "Uncle Prius, I feel that I'm not achieving what I should be achieving at work."

Uncle Prius leaned back in his chair and listened as the Nice Man continued.

"I'm not getting the projects I want. I'm not getting the promotions I deserve. And, quite frankly, I'm not making the money I feel I really could be making, the money I *should* be making – the money I *need* to be making!"

"I see," replied Uncle Prius.

"I'm not in a rut or anything. I just feel that I should be getting more out of all the time I spend at work. I mean, I work eight hours a day, five days a week. That's a lot of time away from my family!"

"I understand very well," Uncle Prius said sympathetically.

"And then on top of all that, I'm just not finding work to be as enjoyable as it once was. Sometimes I'm bored, sometimes I'm frustrated, sometimes I'm just plain aggravated."

"Well," said Uncle Prius, "have you given any thought to what the problem might be?"

"Yes, I have," replied the Nice Man, "and I'm afraid I don't like the answer."

"Which is . . .?"

"Frankly, I think I'm too nice a person to really succeed in the competitive world of business."

"Too nice to succeed in business?" Uncle Prius retorted.

"Yes, too nice. All of the successful businesspeople I know – they have that killer instinct. They have a shark's mentality. I just don't have that. I'm a nice guy, and I don't have what it takes to swim with the sharks. Why, they'll eat me for lunch!"

Uncle Prius ran his hand over his bald head, taking in the Nice Man's story.

"Well," the Nice Man said, shrugging his shoulders, "that's just the way I am. I've always been a nice guy and I'll always be a nice guy. And it seems that nice people finish last in business."

The Nice Man looked down, quite unhappy. "And that's what's holding me back. Being nice is a liability in business, and I'm asking what you would do if you were in my shoes."

Uncle Prius cracked a big smile and let out a hearty laugh.

"My boy, I *was* in your shoes, exactly in your shoes when I was about your age. You see, I'm every bit as nice as you and darn proud of it. Nice to the core and no desire to change."

Uncle Prius leaned forward and looked the Nice Man squarely in the eyes. "Son, being nice in business is not a liability, it's an asset. *In fact, my greatest asset in business is that I am nice, and my greatest achievement in business is figuring out how to Be Nice and Win.*"

"*Be Nice and Win?*" asked the Nice Man.

"That's right," said Uncle Prius. "*Be Nice and Win.* That's the philosophy we follow here at Prius Smith & Co. In fact, all of my top executives started out just like you and me, nice people who were not getting what they wanted out of work. Once they learned about *Be Nice and Win*, that all changed. They became better businesspeople. They worked more effectively, earned more money and had more fun doing so – all because of *Be Nice and Win*."

*My greatest asset in business
is that I am nice,
and my greatest
achievement in business
is figuring out how to
Be Nice and Win.*

"But what does *Be Nice and Win* mean?" asked the Nice Man.

Uncle Prius laughed again. "My boy," he said, "before I tell you what it *means*, you must know what it *is*. And for that, you need some background – a peek into my own business past."

"You see," he continued, "I told you that I'm nice to the core, just like you. And also like you, there was a time when I was not achieving my business goals. I was not getting the fun assignments, I was not being promoted, and I was not earning the money I needed."

"Did you blame it on being too nice, like I do?" asked the Nice Man.

"Well, it was tempting," Uncle Prius replied. "But I knew that there was no sense blaming something that I wasn't going to change. You see, I've always believed that your character and reputation are your two most valuable assets – in business and in life. I didn't want to compromise either of them in any way, shape or form."

"Actually," Uncle Prius continued, "it was not that I was too nice, it was that I was *too busy*! I was so time-deprived that I stopped seeing the forest through the trees."

"What were you doing that made you so busy?" asked the Nice Man.

"Same thing everybody does – I had my work responsibilities, then I had to pay my bills, balance my checkbook, mow the lawn, fix the house, raise the kids – why it's amazing that I had time to breathe!"

"So what did you do?"

Uncle Prius slowly settled back into his thick leather chair, smiled and said: "What I did was I turned to the *experts* for help. I went in search of their advice on *how nice people succeed in business.* I started reading every best-selling business book I could find, books written by very smart and very successful people."

"And?" asked the Nice Man.

"And I never stopped! Just look around you." Uncle Prius pointed to the wall behind the Nice Man, gesturing to the vast array of books. The wall was lined with them, floor to ceiling, stretching clear across the entire office. There were hardcover books, paperback books, old books, new books, books of all colors and sizes.

The Nice Man got up from his seat and went over to the wall, glancing from one title to the next. He had heard of many of them, and had even read quite a few.

"Go ahead and pick out some books that you've read and bring 'em over to me," Uncle Prius said as he walked over to his desk.

The Nice Man started pulling books from the shelves. First one, then a second, then a third. He handed them to Uncle Prius, who made a stack of them on his desk.

"Let's see what you've got so far," said Uncle Prius.

- *How to Win Friends & Influence People* by Dale Carnegie
- *The 7 Habits of Highly Effective People* by Stephen Covey
- *What They Don't Teach You at Harvard Business School* by Mark McCormack
- *The One Minute Manager* by Kenneth Blanchard and Spencer Johnson
- *Who Moved My Cheese?* by Spencer Johnson
- *Think and Grow Rich* by Napoleon Hill
- *Leading with the Heart* by Mike Krzyzewski
- *Success Is a Choice* by Rick Pitino
- *The Power of Positive Thinking* by Norman Vincent Peale
- *Getting to Yes* by Roger Fisher
- *Awaken the Giant Within* by Anthony Robbins

The Nice Man looked proudly at the collection. "I've read all of these," he said.

"Excellent," said Uncle Prius. "And what did you get from them?"

"Why, lots of very interesting advice."

"Indeed," replied Uncle Prius with a bit of a scowl. "*Too much* interesting advice. What I found was that I would read the books and then quickly forget what they taught me! Why, there's only so much information I can cram into this tiny noggin of mine," he said, patting his bald head.

"Well," said the Nice Man, "now that I think about it, I guess you're right. Just looking at the books on your desk, I would be hard-pressed to remember their advice. And I honestly can't say that I've actually used a whole lot of what they taught me."

"And that's too bad," Uncle Prius said as they both sat back down around the coffee table, "because all of that reading and all of that great advice doesn't do a darn thing for you if you don't actually use it!"

Uncle Prius sighed in disappointment at the thought of the experts' advice being lost in its own complexity.

Looking back at the Nice Man, he said: "What I needed was something simpler. I needed expert advice that I could easily remember, advice that I could actually use at work. *I needed simple and practical advice on how nice people succeed in business.*"

What I needed was something simpler. I needed expert advice that I could easily remember, advice that I could actually use at work.

I needed simple and practical advice on how nice people succeed in business.

"And?" the Nice Man prompted him.

"And so I did what always works best – I simplified! I took all of what the experts had to say and I simplified it into a single theme, a theme that the experts all agree on – a theme that became the foundation for my business philosophy *Be Nice and Win*."

The Nice Man moved to the edge of his chair. "What is it?" he asked. "What's the theme?"

Uncle Prius smiled again and in a hushed voice said: "*People – business is all about people.*"

He then paused for effect as the Nice Man contemplated this truth.

"*The experts tell us that success in business, as in life, is all about people and how well we relate to them. Business is a playing field of people, and our success depends on how well we act toward other people, how well we react to them, and how well we interact with them.*"

The Nice Man was quick to agree. "Yes, that's so true! I mean, customers are people and you need customers to buy your goods and services. So your success in business greatly depends on how well you relate to your customers."

"That's right," Uncle Prius responded. "And your bosses are people, and you need to relate well to them because they're the ones who recognize and reward your good work."

Business is all about people.

*Your success in business
depends on how well you act,
react, and interact with others.*

The Nice Man kept it going, saying, "And your colleagues at work are people, and you need to relate well to them because they can make or break you in all kinds of ways!"

"Yes they can," Uncle Prius said with a smile. "You know the old saying, 'Keep your friends close and your enemies closer.'"

"And don't forget your friends and family," said the Nice Man. "You may not work with them, but they're your support group when things at work get tough."

"And while you might not think about it, you also need to relate well to your competitors," added Uncle Prius.

"My competitors?" asked the Nice Man.

"Yes – competitors today, but possibly colleagues tomorrow. You should always keep your options open!"

The Nice Man nodded in agreement. Uncle Prius was quite prescient, he thought. "So," he said, "business is all about people, and success in business is determined by how well you act, react, and interact with them. I agree, but I still don't understand how this helps me. Did the experts offer any *advice* that I can use to improve how I work with others?"

"The experts offer a lot of advice," Prius replied with a smile. "So once again, I simplified. I collected the experts' very best advice, the advice they all agreed on – the *consensus* expert advice – and I simplified it into three easy and effective 'Strategies for Success.'"

"Three easy and effective Strategies for Success?" repeated the Nice Man.

"Yes, strategies that everyone can easily remember and effectively use at work. Strategies that help you hone the skills you need to win at business."

"But how do you know these strategies work?"

Uncle Prius gave another hearty laugh and said, "First of all, they come from time-proven expert advice, the cream-of-the-crop. Remember, I picked the *consensus* expert advice – advice that the experts all agree on."

"An all-star team of advice?"

"Exactly, only simplified into three easy and effective strategies," Uncle Prius replied. "In addition, the three Strategies work because each is *entirely within your control*. They are yours to use however and whenever you wish. If you're firmly committed to success, then there's nothing that stands in your way."

"I like that," the Nice Man replied. "Time-proven consensus expert advice that's entirely within my control."

"And," Uncle Prius continued, "they work because they are high-road strategies that are perfectly suited for nice people. *The strategies work with your natural character and build on your strengths as a nice person*, and that's particularly appealing for nice people who want to succeed in an honest and honorable way."

The three Strategies for Success work because:

1. They are time-proven consensus expert advice;

2. They are entirely within your control; and

3. They work with your natural character and build on your strengths as a nice person.

"So, *Be Nice and Win* is about three Strategies for Success based on time-proven consensus expert advice, strategies that are entirely within my control and that build on my strengths as a nice person."

"That's exactly right," replied Uncle Prius, smiling and nodding his head in approval. "*Be Nice and Win* is about how nice people succeed in business."

"That sounds good to me," the Nice Man said. "So what are the three Strategies for Success?"

Uncle Prius laughed. "My boy," he said, "you've already learned a lot today. Why don't you come by my office tomorrow morning and I'll introduce you to Sam, my director of personnel. Sam's one of us – a nice guy who wanted more from work. I took him in ten years ago and mentored him in *Be Nice and Win*. Sam can tell you all about it."

"That would be great," said the Nice Man.

The Nice Man was intrigued by what he had heard. Three easy and effective Strategies for Success, each culled from the consensus advice of expert businesspeople as told in their best-selling business books. Three strategies that are entirely within his control and, most importantly, work with his natural character and build on his strengths as a nice person.

He thought about Uncle Prius and the many business books he has read through the years, searching for expert advice on how nice people succeed in business. He also thought about his own experiences with business books, how they offered so much advice that he ended up using very little of it. Uncle Prius was right – you have to make things simple to make them to work.

He thought about the simple premise behind *Be Nice and Win* – that business is all about people. He thought about how success in business is greatly impacted by how well you relate to other people, how well you act, react, and interact with them.

He also thought about the high-road to success. Like Uncle Prius, he did not want to compromise his values in his pursuit of success. Rather, he was excited about building on his strengths as a nice person, and he looked forward to tomorrow when he would learn how.

The Nice Man returned to Uncle Prius' office early the next morning.

"Good morning, Nancy," the Nice Man said to Uncle Prius' assistant.

"Good morning to you," she replied with a smile. "I'll let Prius know you're here. He's in with Sam right now."

Nancy picked up the phone and rang Prius. "He said to go right in," she said, waving him on.

The Nice Man walked past her desk and opened Uncle Prius' office door.

"Come in, come in my good boy," Uncle Prius said. "Allow me to introduce you to Sam, our director of personnel."

"Hello, Sam. It's a pleasure to meet you," the Nice Man said as they shook hands.

"I was just telling Sam that you are interested in learning *Be Nice and Win*'s three Strategies for Success."

"I certainly am," the Nice Man said with excitement.

"Well," said Sam, "I'm just the person you want. Prius here taught me everything I know about business, and it all started with *Be Nice and Win*."

"What did you do before you joined Prius Smith & Co.?" asked the Nice Man.

"I was an unhappy salesman for a large electronics firm," replied Sam. "I wasn't making the sales that I needed to make. I wasn't hitting my numbers, and that got me frustrated and upset – which hurt my sales even more!"

"That sounds terrible," said the Nice Man.

"It was, I assure you," replied Sam. "But then I took the initiative and cold-called your uncle Prius."

"You cold-called Uncle Prius, the head of Prius Smith & Co.?" asked the Nice Man.

"Sure. I had just read an article in the newspaper about how nice a person Prius was, so I picked up the phone and called him. He took the call and, after talking for a few minutes, told me that I was very brave to cold-call the president of a large company. That made me feel very good. And he invited me in to visit him."

"And what happened then?"

"Well, he got to asking me whether I liked my job, and I just broke down – told him everything right here in this very office – how I was frustrated, upset and not making the money I needed to make."

"Sounds like me," said the Nice Man.

"Yes, and that's when he told me about *Be Nice and Win* – about the experts' consensus advice that business is all about people and that success comes to those who work best with other people, and about the three Strategies for Success. Since then, my life has turned around completely. I love my job, I love the people I work with, and I look forward to going to work every day."

"And you make a pretty penny when you do," added Uncle Prius with a wink.

"Yes, my compensation certainly has gone up, as have the profits at Prius Smith & Co.!" Sam said with a nod back to Prius, who is never shy about crediting his business growth to *Be Nice and Win*. "And that's because of the energy and enthusiasm I now have for my work, energy and enthusiasm that came with my understanding of how to *Be Nice and Win*."

"And that's what you're going to show me?" asked the Nice Man, leading him on.

"Yes he will," replied Uncle Prius. "Why don't we all take the elevator down to the conference room floor where you and Sam can get settled in and talk shop."

The three men left Prius' office and walked over to the elevator. As they arrived, the elevator door opened and a short, balding man in his mid-thirties stepped out. The man seemed quite upset. He saw Prius and strutted right up to him.

"Prius," he said in an angry voice, "you have some nerve."

"Why George, what's the matter?"

"As if you don't know," George grumbled. "Have you seen the price of gas recently? Have you?"

George was flailing his arms and turning red in the face. "Gas is now over $3 a gallon. It's gone from $2 to over $3 since we started doing your deliveries. Prius, we're supposed to be 50-50 partners in this deal, but my company is getting shortchanged. We're taking huge losses delivering products for you while you make all the money. That's not what I call 50-50 partners."

Prius was about to interrupt, but he stepped back instead and let George continue. The Nice Man and Sam looked at each other, and then back at George.

"You think you can get away with this because you're the famous Prius Smith, but not with me. Not with my company. Why, my family's business has been profitable ever since we started 75 years ago, and we've worked with far bigger people than you – Henry Ford at Ford Motor Company, Ray Kroc at McDonald's, Bill Hewlett and Dave Packard at Hewlett Packard. In fact, this dog of a deal with Prius Smith & Co. is our only loser!"

George was getting madder by the minute.

"And I'm not going to take it. I want you to cancel the deal right now. No more delivering your product at a loss while you make all the money."

"Well George," said Prius with a sigh, "I'm sorry you feel that way, and I certainly understand your frustrations. No one likes to lose money."

"So the deal is off?"

Prius gave George a very stern stare, looking him right in the eye, and replied, "No, it's not."

George backed off a bit and said: "Well then, how do you propose to fix our broken deal?"

"George," Prius said, putting his arm on the man's shoulder, "Prius Smith & Co. can't earn a profit on our product if we can't get it to market, and you're our first and only choice for delivery. You're the best there is, and no one is even a close second."

"Damn straight," George replied, fixing his tie and seeming a little calmer and a lot more collected.

"And we know that we'll make money on this product well past this temporary surge in gas prices. So here's what I'll do. Prius Smith & Co. will reimburse you for all gas costs above $2, the cost of gas when we signed our deal. That will get you through this and also allow us to continue to get our product to market."

George still seemed a bit miffed, but he was now gratified that he could get back to profitability. "Well, I guess that would be satisfactory," he said.

"In fact," Prius continued, "I'll have the contract amendment drawn up and I will personally visit with your father for his signature. I will be sure to tell him how concerned you were with protecting the family business."

The Nice Man thought he saw a smile briefly appear on George's lips. "That would be very good of you," George said gruffly, not entirely sure what to say. "I hope that we'll never have such a terrible and unforeseeable event like this again."

"Why don't you come on back to my office and we can work up that amendment," offered Prius as he patted George on the back. "Sam, why don't the two of you go on down to the conference room together and meet me back in my office around four."

"Sure thing, boss," said Sam as he and the Nice Man got into the open elevator and went down to the conference room floor.

"That Prius," said Sam as the elevator door closed, "he's the absolute master of people skills."

"Why do you say that?" asked the Nice Man.

"Why, the way he handled George," replied Sam. "He uses *Be Nice and Win* like no one else."

"Huh?" replied the Nice Man. "All I saw was that he caved in to a grown man throwing a temper tantrum."

Sam laughed. "To you it seems like he caved in, but you'll soon realize that he was actually the winner."

The elevator door opened and Sam led the Nice Man into the first conference room on the floor, the Board Room.

"How did he win?" asked the Nice Man. "Why, he willingly conceded to George that he would cover the gas losses, and that costs him real money!"

"A good point," said Sam as he closed the door, "and I'll explain it all. But why don't we start at the top. Tell me what Prius has already told you about *Be Nice and Win*."

They both sat down at the large conference table.

"He told me that *Be Nice and Win* is derived from the consensus advice of business experts on how nice people succeed in business, and that it simplifies the advice so that we can actually remember it and use it at work – making it easy and effective."

"Good," said Sam. "And what else did he say?"

"He said that *Be Nice and Win* has a single premise – that business is all about people, and that success comes to those who work well with other people."

"You have an excellent memory! I can see that you will master *Be Nice and Win* in a short time," said Sam.

The compliment made the Nice Man feel good. "And," the Nice Man continued, "he said that *Be Nice and Win* has three Strategies for Success, strategies that are also derived from the experts' consensus advice and that build on my strengths as a nice person."

"Well done!" said Sam. "Why don't we start then with the first strategy. You should know that your uncle Prius just gave you a wonderful performance of this first strategy."

"He did?" replied the Nice Man. "During George's silly temper tantrum?"

"Yes. You see, the first strategy of *Be Nice and Win* goes right to the core of people skills, of working with others one-to-one, even with people like George. We call this first strategy EMPATHY."

Sam let the Nice Man think about this for a moment as he poured a glass of water for each of them.

"Empathy is about understanding people," Sam continued. "It's about putting yourself in other people's shoes and seeing the world from their perspective. It's about understanding how they feel, what they see, and how they think."

"You learned that business is all about people, about how you act, react, and interact with them. Well, to succeed in business you need to hone your people skills, skills that help you truly understand the people you work with."

"That makes sense," said the Nice Man. "My father is a divorce lawyer and he's always saying that the main reason people end their marriages is that they just don't understand their spouses very well."

Sam nodded. "Whether in marriage or business, the better you understand the other person, the better you can relate to them. Now, *Be Nice and Win* divides Empathy into two parts. It tells us that to truly Empathize with people *you need to understand them for what they are, and also for what they are doing.*"

"I don't understand the difference," replied the Nice Man.

"*Understanding people for what they are* is about character analysis, figuring out what type of person they are so you can understand and relate to them better," explained Sam. "*Understanding people for what they are doing* is a situational analysis. It's about figuring out what the person is really feeling, really saying, really doing at a given moment."

STRATEGY FOR SUCCESS #1

EMPATHY

Empathy is about understanding people.
It's about understanding them for what they are,
and for what they are doing.

✦

Sam continued: "Let's first take a closer look at character analysis – *understanding people for what they are.* The importance of this is that people fall into different character types, and each character type requires a different style of action, reaction and interaction. You need to understand the character types, how to peg people within them, and then how to adjust your behavior accordingly."

"Okay," said the Nice Man. "So how do I do that?"

"Well," Sam replied, "the experts offer a lot of wonderful advice about character analysis and present us with many types of characters and ways to relate to them. Some of the advice is very detailed and complicated, but with *Be Nice and Win* we want advice that's easy and effective, advice that we can actually remember and use at work."

"I presume Prius has some in mind?" asked the Nice Man.

"A good guess," chuckled Sam. "Prius is quite fond of a character analysis based on one of his books – *People Styles at Work* by Robert Bolton and Dorothy Grover Bolton."

"How does this character analysis work?" asked the Nice Man.

"It defines character based on 'Assertiveness' and 'Responsiveness.' Assertiveness means the degree to which people see you as being forceful and directive. Responsiveness means the degree to which they see you as being emotional and caring."

"So Assertiveness is 'results-focused' and Responsiveness is 'people-focused?'"

"Exactly," replied Sam. "It then defines four character styles, each based on their degree of Assertiveness and Responsiveness."

"What are they?"

"The first one is called Analytical. Analyticals are in the bottom half of both Assertiveness and Responsiveness – not very results-focused or people-focused. They tend to be detail-oriented people, very systematic and organized. Analyticals love information and will gather as much of it as possible before making a decision. Their offices are often piled high with books, reports and other information they've collected."

"Sounds like my accountant," replied the Nice Man. "Great with numbers and information, but not exactly a people person."

Sam nodded in agreement. "Detail-oriented professions appeal to Analyticals, and you'll see many of them as accountants, librarians, statisticians and scientists."

"Then there's the Amiable," Sam continued. "Amiables are low Assertiveness and high Responsiveness – not very results-focused but highly people-focused. Relationships are key to Amiables. They enjoy working in groups and helping others, and prefer doing business with friends and people they trust – you'll find lots of pictures of family and friends in the Amiable's office. Amiables are more emotional and caring than Analyticals, but like Analyticals they are not very results-focused."

"My wife is definitely an Amiable," the Nice Man said. "She's always gravitating toward people she likes and trusts, yet just can't seem to get things done on time."

Sam chuckled. "Next is the Expressive, a true people person. Expressives are highly results-focused and also highly people-focused. They are often flamboyant leader types with abundant energy. Expressives think and plan in broad strokes, seek out the limelight and love to hold court. They host lunches, make speeches and announce great plans, but let others attend to the details."

"What will I find in the Expressive's office?"

"You'll often find pictures of the Expressive with celebrities, sports stars, politicians and the like," replied Sam.

"I have a friend who's a real estate developer," the Nice Man said. "He sounds just like an Expressive – always slapping backs, promoting his projects and telling you about his latest celebrity encounter."

"Finally," Sam said, "there's the Driver. Drivers are highly results-focused and not at all people-focused. They have a practicality and bottom-line orientation, are very decisive, but not very caring about others. While the Analytical is thinking about a problem, the Amiable is meeting on it and the Expressive is talking about it, the Driver will be doing something about it. Drivers often make mistakes because of their impulsiveness, but they are also quick to change their course and make up for them."

"And in the Driver's office?"

"The Driver's office is usually spotless. The desk is organized and clean, pictures are properly aligned on shelves, not too much paperwork evident and not too much clutter."

"Sounds like my boss, the founder and president of our company."

"Yes," Sam replied, "entrepreneurs and CEOs are often Drivers. Now, people can have two traits – a primary trait and a secondary trait. For example, you can be an Expressive Amiable, someone who is an Amiable at heart but with Expressive tendencies. But that's something you don't need to learn about right now."

"Okay, so how does all this help me?" asked the Nice Man. "How do I work better with people once I've pegged their character type?"

"To work well with a Driver," Sam said, "you need to keep things short and sweet. Give him only the top-line relevant information. He's not interested in the nitty-gritty, just the skinny. He'll leave the rest up to you."

"Sounds like a good person to work for," commented the Nice Man.

"Yes, if you deliver," said Sam. "And if you don't, the Driver is not that interested in your excuses – doesn't care that much for details, or other people for that matter."

"Hmmm," replied the Nice Man, shaking his head in cautious contemplation.

"The best way to work with an Expressive is to play to his ego. Let him talk. Listen and smile. Keep in mind that Expressives tend to be whimsical, so you'll need to be flexible and roll with their punches."

"Okay," said the Nice Man. "And what about the Analytical?"

"To work well with an Analytical you need to answer all of his questions and supply him with all of the information he needs. Never pressure him to make a decision until he has finished his analysis. Analyticals can be demanding and trying, but once they do their research and are comfortable with their conclusion, they rarely waver."

"And the Amiable?"

"To work well with an Amiable you need to become his friend before doing anything else. You need to forge a personal bond and work hard to maintain it. Once that bond is there, the Amiable will trust you and your work with him will be much easier and smoother."

The Nice Man thought about the four character types and the best ways to work with each. "What happens if you don't respect their characters, if you treat them all the same?" he asked.

"Very bad, very bad," said Sam. "Tell a Driver too much and he will not want to speak to you anymore. Tell an Analytical too little and he won't want to speak to you either. Tell an Amiable the wrong thing . . .."

"I get the picture," the Nice Man said, holding up his hands. "So, Empathy is about understanding people for what they are, which means identifying their character type and adjusting my behavior accordingly. And since business is all about people, the better the relationships I can forge, the more success I'll achieve."

"That's right," said Sam. "Your uncle Prius is a genius in character analysis. He can peg someone in a very short time. We normal people take a bit longer. But once we get it, once we can identify someone's character, it makes working with them so much easier, so much more effective and so much more fun!"

"So what about George?" asked the Nice Man. "How would you peg George?"

"Well," said Sam, looking up and thinking, "I would say George is an Expressive. Remember when he was rattling off all those people his family has worked with – Hewlett, Packard, Ford, Kroc? I'll bet George's office is filled with pictures of him with celebrities. That's an Expressive for you."

"And so that's why Uncle Prius let George keep yelling at him, and then buttered him up. He let the Expressive talk, and then played to his ego."

"That's part of it," replied Sam. "Prius' actions also beautifully demonstrated the second part of Empathy, which is *understanding people for what they are doing*. But before you learn this part of Empathy, I need to make an important phone call, so if you'll excuse me for a few minutes. . ."

Sam left the room and the Nice Man contemplated what he had learned so far about Empathy, about *understanding people for what they are* – their character type.

The Nice Man agreed that this was an easy and effective way to hone his people skills, and he was excited about trying it out and having fun pegging people as Driver, Expressive, Amiable, or Analytical. He knew that everyone didn't fit perfectly into one of the four molds, and that he would get better at pegging them with time and practice.

The Nice Man also thought about how important it is to interact with people according to their character type. Even the smallest nuances could make dramatic differences to different people. He would be mistaken to be curt with an Analytical, while that same approach can work wonders with a Driver. An Expressive would be tickled pink if he kept quiet and lent a willing ear, while that tack would fall on its face with an Amiable.

The Nice Man knew that these skills would be very effective at work, helping him to forge new relationships and strengthen existing ones. And since business is all about people, that means success.

A few minutes after he left, Sam opened the conference room door and strode inside. "I'm back," he said. "Sorry about that."

"That's okay," said the Nice Man. "It gave me a chance to think about the four character types."

"Now remember," said Sam, "that's just one way to analyze character types and hone your people skills. There are others out there, but Prius feels that this one is the easiest and most effective. He's always saying, '*To be effective it's got to be memorable, and to be memorable it's got to be easy.*'"

The Nice Man laughed, as he could see his uncle Prius saying exactly that.

"Now," Sam continued, "let's go back and look at the encounter between your uncle Prius and George, and the second part of Empathy – *understanding people for what they are doing.*"

"I know exactly what George was doing – he was acting like a spoiled brat," the Nice Man responded.

"On the surface, yes," Sam said, "but to understand people for what they are doing you need to get below the surface, you need to understand what they are really feeling, really thinking."

"And how do I do that?" asked the Nice Man.

"Again, there are lots of expert systems for doing so, but we stick to the simple and practical. We call our system '*collect, correct, and confirm.*'"

"'Collect, correct, and confirm' – easy enough to remember. How does it work?"

"'Collect' is about taking in the critical information you need to figure out what people are really feeling, really saying, really thinking. It's about observing other people when they're talking to you."

Sam continued: "According to the experts, up to 85% of our communication is nonverbal. Just think about that for a minute – *the words you hear are only about 15% of the message the speaker sends you.*"

This took the Nice Man by surprise. He had never stopped to think about how important nonverbal factors are in figuring out a person's true message. Even if it was less than 85%, even if it was 60% or even 40%, it is still a substantial part of the message. "I never realized how much we could learn from nonverbal communications! How can I 'collect' that information?"

"You've got to observe it, and to observe it you've got to focus, and to focus you've go to stop doing what so many people do – *plotting your response while the other person is still talking.*"

The Nice Man chuckled, saying, "Oh, am I ever guilty of that! I do it all the time, and you're right – I'm so preoccupied figuring out my own response that I don't really focus on the other person. I don't really 'observe' like I should."

"It's a bad habit that we all have," Sam agreed. "So next time you speak to someone, take a mental step back and train your brain on the other person's nonverbal communications."

"Such as?"

"Such as their facial expression. You'll get a world of insight into what a speaker is truly feeling and saying if you stop plotting your response and focus instead on changes in his facial expression. Pay particular attention to the eyes – the eyes are an open window to a person's thoughts and feelings!"

"I once heard Uncle Prius say 'The eyes never lie.'"

Sam laughed. "That's very true. And also focus on vocal tones. Vocal tones give you great clues to what is meant by what is said."

"Everyone knows that!" said the Nice Man.

"Sure, and most everyone can tell from the vocal tone whether 'What a day I had' means a good day or a bad one. It's when the message is subtler that you really have to focus. For example, if your customer says, 'Sure, I understand that you have to raise your prices to reflect cost increases,' how do you know if he's truly accepting your price increase, or if he is mad at you and plans to take his business elsewhere?"

"I don't know," replied the Nice Man with some uncertainty.

"That's why you need to stop plotting and start focusing. A speaker's speed, volume and pitch offer critical clues to her hidden meaning."

"Now that sounds hard to do, and you said that 'collect, correct, and confirm' is easy!"

"It is easy, and you'll find that it gets easier and easier once you get yourself to stop plotting and start focusing on the nuances. The hard part isn't understanding the nuances, it's training yourself to observe them! It might feel a bit forced at first, but with time your observation skills will become second nature and they'll give you a valuable advantage in business."

"How else can I collect information in addition to observing rather than plotting?"

"Another very helpful way to get information is to simply *let other people talk*. Don't interrupt them. Bite your lip, let them rant on. The more they talk, the more they tell you, the more information you collect and the better you can assess what they are truly saying. Do you remember when George had just started yelling at Prius, and you and I looked at each other?"

"I do," replied the Nice Man.

"Right there at the beginning, it looked as if Prius was going to cut George off and toss him out on his rear, right?"

"Yes! And that's what he should have done," replied the Nice Man. "I've always been taught that there's no reason to reprimand or demean people, especially in front of others."

"That's true," said Sam, "but Prius didn't stop him. Instead, he let George talk away. Prius wanted information so he could see beyond George's temper tantrum and figure out what was really bothering him."

"Interrupting people has become so common that we don't even think about," replied the Nice Man. "I was always taught not to interrupt because it's rude, but as you point out it also stops the flow of important information."

The Nice Man thought about this for a bit and then added: "But what if the other person is not as cooperative as George? What if the other person is not inclined to talk?"

"Help him," replied Sam. "Have you ever tried offering someone a dose of silence?"

"No."

"Well, silence is a great way to get people talking. Just stare at them a bit and put the onus to talk on them. Most people hate that awkward break in conversation and they'll start talking out of impulse. It's a great way to get information."

"You mean just stare at them?"

"Yes, or you can encourage them to talk with short and leading questions. That will keep the conversation on the track you want while also getting them to talk and provide the information you need."

Sam took a sip of water and smiled. "Getting information from people is so important, and it's second nature to *Be Nice and Win* masters like your uncle Prius. Why, other people have no idea that he's eliciting important information simply by listening, which is just as well because you get better information that way. It's an absolute treat to watch your uncle Prius in action!"

"Okay, so then what information did Uncle Prius get from George that was so important?"

"If you remember," Sam responded, "George ranted on about his family business being profitable for 75 years, and that his deal with Prius Smith & Co. was the only deal they had where they were losing money – the deal that George himself negotiated!"

"So what? All that tells me is that George made a bad business deal and Prius made a good one."

"Yes, well, the next part of 'collect, correct and confirm' is to correct how we interpret the information we've collected. The experts tell us that people tend to err in their interpretation of what others are communicating because they see things from their own perspective. *What we need to do is interpret the information from the other person's perspective, to put ourselves in their shoes and listen to their message from their point of view.*"

"And how does that help you with George?"

"Well, think about what George said from George's perspective. Here we have young George in a family business that's been around for 75 years, and profitable for each one. The burden is on his shoulders to continue that streak, to fill the shoes of his father and grandfather. Now, here's this great deal that he sealed with Prius Smith & Co., one of the state's biggest companies. A deal George probably touted in front of his father and his family to prove how good he is – and bam, gas prices spike, he's losing money, and he's looking real foolish in front of his family."

"I guess I never really thought of it that way," replied the Nice Man. "Instead of being mad at George, I kind of feel sorry for him."

Sam smiled. "You see how your interpretation changes when you change your perspective! You get a whole different message, a whole different meaning to a person's words."

Your interpretation changes
when you change your perspective.

You get a whole different message,
a whole different meaning
to a person's words.

"Okay," said the Nice Man, "I understand 'collect and correct,' but how do I then 'confirm'? After all, I'm not psychic!"

"You don't have to be psychic," Sam chuckled, "because *Be Nice and Win* gives you an easy and effective way to confirm your interpretation of their message. You simply ask the other person."

"Ask him? Isn't that a bit odd?"

"Not when you do it right, the way the experts suggest. If you feel the need to confirm that you're reading the message correctly, the experts advise you to *paraphrase – to offer a concise response stating the essence of their message in your own words.*"

Sam continued: "Note the three operative parts: 'concise,' 'essence,' and 'your own words.' You don't need to expound in detail, you don't need to hark on every thought, and you don't need to regurgitate their words. Simply offer a summary of the overall message as you get it, in your own words."

"So," the Nice Man paraphrased with a touch of humor, "we can understand people for what they are doing by listening and observing better, and we do that by 'collect, correct, and confirm' – letting them talk, even encouraging them to talk, and observing their nonverbal messages."

Sam smiled and added: "*Stop* what you're doing, *look* at them when they're talking, *and listen* to their nonverbal message. It's really easy once you get the hang of it."

"So how did all of this end up helping Prius?" asked the Nice Man.

"Prius had a business decision to make: cancel George's contract and throw him out, or not. It would have been easy for him to just cancel the contract and toss him out, but easy isn't always best. To succeed in business, you need to make the *right* decisions. And by taking the time to understand what George was really thinking, really saying to him, Prius was able to make the best decision and solidify what will undoubtedly prove to be a great relationship."

The Nice Man could clearly see how he had misinterpreted George's tirade, even George himself. If he were in Uncle Prius' position, he would have made the wrong business decision because he did not truly understand George or George's message.

Now he understood the importance of observing others – to "collect, correct, and confirm" their nonverbal message. He understood the importance of letting people talk, even encouraging them to talk. He understood the importance of putting aside his own biases and seeing things from the other person's perspective. Finally, he understood how to confirm his interpretation by concisely paraphrasing the essence of the message in his own words.

Sam smiled and said, "Character styles will help you understand people for what they are. 'Collect, correct and confirm' will help you understand people for what they are doing. That's all you'll need to hone your people skills, to perfect how you act, react and interact with people in one-to-one situations. And they are both totally within your control – skills that you can use whenever you please."

"And like Uncle Prius said," the Nice Man replied, "they are high-road skills that work with my natural character and build on my strengths as a nice person. Nice people should welcome the opportunity to better understand the people we work with, to better Empathize with them."

"And you'll find that the better *you* understand *them*, the better *they* will want to understand *you*. Empathy is a two-way street, and your path to success becomes much easier when you have other people helping you along!"

EMPATHY

Understand people for what they are ...
- Drivers
- Expressives
- Amiables
- Analyticals

... and for what they are doing.
- Collect
  - Don't plot while they speak
  - Observe the nonverbal message
  - Let them talk, encourage it
- Correct
  - Think from their perspective
- Confirm
  - Concisely paraphrase the essence of the message

Just then, there was a knock on the conference room door. Sam went over and opened it.

"Hi Sam," a man said. "I thought I saw you go in here earlier."

"Hi Tim, come on in," said Sam. Tim, the sales director for Prius Smith & Co., entered the Board Room and Sam made the introductions.

"This young lad is learning all about *Be Nice and Win* and its three Strategies for Success," Sam said, "and we just finished discussing Empathy."

"Excellent," replied Tim, smiling at the Nice Man. "Your uncle Prius made all the difference in my business career, I'll tell you that. Once I started practicing *Be Nice and Win* my attitude toward work changed entirely. Now I have much more fun and make a lot more money than before!"

"I have a few phone calls to make," Sam said. "Tim, would you like to take over for me and continue with the second strategy?"

"It would be my pleasure," replied Tim. Turning to the Nice Man, he said, "Why don't you join me in the next conference room, the Sales Room. Our sales teams are meeting in there right now."

"Your sales teams?" asked the Nice Man. "Do all of your salespeople work in teams?"

"Sure do," replied Tim. "Feeds right into the charm of *Be Nice and Win*. But before we go, tell me – what have you learned so far?"

"I've learned that *Be Nice and Win* has a single premise – that business is all about people. It's a team sport, and the better we act, react, and interact with other people, the better businesspeople we become."

"That's right," said Tim. "What else?"

"I learned that *Be Nice and Win* has three Strategies for Success. Each strategy is easy to remember and easy to use at work. And the strategies are all what Uncle Prius calls high-road strategies that are perfectly suited for nice people like me – building on my strengths as a nice person."

"So far, so good," smiled Tim. "What else?"

"The first strategy is Empathy. Empathy is about understanding people, lots of people – customers, colleagues, bosses, family, friends, and even competitors. It's about understanding them for what they are, and for what they are doing. The better we understand other people, the better we can act, react, and interact with them – and that leads to success."

"That's right," said Tim.

"*Understanding people for what they are* is about character types. You need to identify a person's character type and then adjust your behavior accordingly. Sam told me about Drivers, Expressives, Analyticals and Amiables. He taught me how to peg people within those four character types, and how to work best with each."

"What else?" asked Tim.

"To *understand people for what they are doing*," the Nice Man continued, "you need to get inside their head and find their hidden message. We do that with a system called 'collect, correct, and confirm.'"

"Excellent!" Tim exclaimed. "I can see that you're going to master *Be Nice and Win* in no time!"

Once again the Nice Man felt proud at the compliment. He enjoyed being nice to others, and he enjoyed when others were nice to him.

"Sam said that you could teach me the second *Be Nice and Win* Strategy for Success," the Nice Man said, eager to learn more.

"I'd be delighted to," replied Tim. "Why don't we jump next door to the Sales Room and meet the sales teams while we explore the second strategy – what we call SYNERGY."

Tim and the Nice Man left the Board Room and went next door to the Sales Room, an even larger conference room where several dozen people were milling about in small groups.

"Okay, everyone, let's settle down. We have a special guest with us, a nice young man who is learning *Be Nice and Win*. He already knows all about Empathy and is now ready to learn about the second Strategy for Success – SYNERGY."

"Well, you certainly came to the right place," said a smiling woman toward the front. "Our sales teams are the very definition of Synergy."

The Nice Man interjected: "May I ask why you do all of your selling in teams? Wouldn't you cover more ground if you worked individually?"

"Yes we would," replied the woman, "but covering more ground doesn't necessarily lead to more sales. You see, we strive for results, and what *Be Nice and Win* teaches us – what the second strategy of Synergy demonstrates – is that we can sell more and accomplish more when we work in teams, when we Synergize."

An older woman on the same sales team broke in: "*Synergy, young man, means achieving more as a group than you would individually. It means teamwork. It means making the team work, and making it work for you.*"

STRATEGY FOR SUCCESS #2

SYNERGY

*Synergy means achieving more as a group
than you would individually.
It means teamwork.
It means making the team work,
and making it work for you.*

A gentleman from a different team jumped in: "So, Empathy is about getting the most you can from people, and Synergy is about getting the most you can from teams – the leveraged results of people working together. Both are critical parts of the *Be Nice and Win* premise that business is all about people, that it's a playing field of people. Empathy focuses on one-to-one people skills, and Synergy focuses on teamwork skills."

The Nice Man had spent the morning thinking about one-to-one people skills, and he was not yet thinking about larger-group interactions. "How large do the groups have to be to achieve Synergy?" he asked.

"Why, they can be as small as two people," the gentleman responded. "Two people can make a team, and the Synergy skills we learn with *Be Nice and Win* apply just as well to groups of two as they do to 200."

"And Synergy applies not only to defined groups such as sales teams, but to less-defined groups as well," the woman added. "Something as simple as a businesswoman and her assistant compose a 'group' that will benefit from the skills of Synergy. It's up to you to 'see the team' in all of your relationships, both business and personal."

"But I already know a lot about 'group skills,'" the Nice Man said. "I'm already very good with organizational behavior issues such as who people report to, the exact nature of the assignment, the tools and budget available, and so forth."

"*Be Nice and Win* Synergy skills are different," the older woman replied. "They focus on people. Our Synergy skills work to optimize teamwork by improving the way the team members act, react, and interact with each other. It's all about the people, and that's because business is all about people."

"You can find great examples of Synergy from successful basketball coaches," said Tim, an avid sports fan. "Coaches like Mike Krzyzewski, Phil Jackson and Rick Pitino are masters at Empathizing with their players individually, and then Synergizing with them as a team for optimal team performance."

"In fact," the gentleman interjected, "the people skills you learned for Empathy will greatly impact Synergy. While Synergy is about optimal teamwork, its roots are in understanding people – and that comes from Empathy! The better you Empathize with your teammates, the better you will understand everyone on the team, and the more Synergy you will create as a result."

"And I presume that the Synergy skills are easy and effective, just like the Empathy skills?"

"Yes they are!" the gentleman exclaimed.

"Okay, so where do we start? How do we make the team work, *and* work for me?" the Nice Man asked.

"Why, I'm not the best person to answer that," the gentleman replied. "Tim there, he's our sales director. He's the teacher. He's the one who can answer that best."

Tim smiled, turned to the Nice Man and said, "Well, there you have the first skill."

The Nice Man was confused. "I don't get it," he said.

The first skill of Synergizing is to *identify the strengths of each team member and then make sure they get work that best fits their strengths.* By recognizing each member's strengths and allocating team tasks accordingly, you get the best team members in any given area using their strengths to achieve the best possible results for the team."

"For example," Tim continued, "you asked that gentleman to explain the Synergy skills. Being well-trained in *Be Nice and Win*, his immediate response was to assign the task to the team's strongest member, which in this room happens to be me, the sales director."

"One thing I've learned after all my years in business is that everyone has strengths and weaknesses. It's just human nature. Some people are good organizers while others can't organize for their life. Some people excel at public speaking while others tremble at the thought of it. Some people enjoy small talk while others are more the quiet type."

"Like me," said the Nice Man, "but just because I'm a bit quiet doesn't mean I'm not nice!"

"Not at all," Tim assured him. "Nice people come in all types. I know a terrific public speaker, a truly nice man, who is just not at all comfortable in one-to-one conversations. He stumbles and bumbles face-to-face, but when he's on stage he's a born leader!"

"So the first skill of Synergizing," said the Nice Man, "is to identify the strengths of everyone on the team and then make sure that people are assigned tasks that best use their strengths. That way, the team gets the best results from its teamwork."

"*Almost* the best results," replied Tim.

"What did I miss?" asked the Nice Man.

"You missed the second skill of Synergy, which is to *align everyone's interests.*"

"And what does that mean?" asked the Nice Man.

"Well, let's say that each team member's skills have been well-defined and team tasks are being assigned accordingly to the strongest team members. Now, let's say that one of those team members is a saleswoman who works on commission, and she stands to earn $150,000 commission from a particular sale."

"That's pretty impressive!" exclaimed the Nice Man.

"It is to her," replied Tim, smiling. "Now, let's say that she's working on a complicated sale that requires lots of filings with the government. But our saleswoman is not concerned because she knows that two other members of her sales team are experts in government filings. They've been doing these filings for years."

"Seems like she has a well-oiled team," replied the Nice Man.

"Not quite," said Tim. "You see, both of these 'experts' are salaried employees making $45,000 a year. Sure, they know how to file, but I can assure you that their hearts are not in it like that of the saleswoman."

"You mean," the Nice Man added, "that because their wallets are not in it, their hearts are not in it – their interests are not aligned."

"That's precisely what I mean," smiled Tim. "So, one of them knows that a filing is due the next morning but he has tickets to the World Series that night. What do you think he's going to do – miss the game to complete the filing, or let the filing slide and hope for the best?"

"Let it slide," replied the Nice Man.

"Sure bet," said Tim.

The Nice Man took over. "But," he said, "suppose the saleswoman promised each of them a $9,000 bonus if the deal closes and every filing had been done timely and accurately. That's a 20% bonus for each just for doing their jobs well, jobs at which they are experts!"

"Now you've got it," said Tim. "She pays them $18,000, and keeps $132,000. Everyone is motivated, everyone is happy, and the deal gets done because everyone's interests are aligned."

"Unaligned interests is a stealth killer," Tim continued. "It's not like a member of the group jumps up and screams, 'Our interests are not aligned!' It's something you have to think about and catch on your own."

"Does 'aligning interests' always involve money?" asked the Nice Man.

"Not at all," said a woman from one of the sales teams. "Bill and I," she said, pointing to one of her teammates, "we have an agreement. Bill has his daughter's wedding next month and he doesn't want any sales to be closing during that time – keep the pressure off him on the big day! So we made a deal that if we work double hard to get our open sales closed before then, he would give me a week out of his vacation time. He gets a great wedding, and I get an extra week off. We've aligned our interests in a mutually beneficial way, and I know that we can get there!"

"That's right," Bill agreed. "It'll be tough, but Shelly and I are sure that we can work hard enough to get those open sales closed before the wedding day."

"And that takes us into another Synergy skill," said Tim.

"What's that?" asked the Nice Man.

"*Always have a positive attitude*," replied Tim.

"That's an easy skill," said the Nice Man. "Everyone knows that the experts advise us to think positively!"

"Perhaps," replied Tim, "but few people actually do it! A lot of lip service is paid to positive attitude, but when the going gets tough, when people are forced to stretch their goals and work under pressure, it takes a lot of strength to keep a smile on your face and a positive attitude toward success."

A portly man in the middle of the room interjected: "What I do to keep a positive attitude is I envision success."

The man shuffled about in his chair, pushed up his glasses, and continued. "Whenever I go on a sales call, when I'm sitting in the waiting room, I envision in my mind what a successful meeting will look like. I envision myself presenting the sale in a clear and concise manner, answering the client's questions and doing what I can to get the client interested. I then envision the client shaking my hand and agreeing to buy. I can always see the happiness in the client's eyes when he makes the buy. To me, that's success. And by envisioning success I can keep a positive attitude all the way through the meeting, even when things get tough – as they invariably do."

The Nice Man had heard of visualization before. "I read that athletes do that, too," he said. "They envision a successful pitch before they throw, a successful drive before they swing."

"That's exactly right," replied the portly man. "Business-people can learn a lot from athletes."

"And perhaps that's why Bob's sales team is our number-one producer!" added Tim, nodding at the portly man. Bob smiled back at the compliment.

"Or it could be that he gets the best territory," said a woman from a different sales team in a somewhat snide manner.

"Now, now, Karen," Tim said. "Perhaps you can explain to our nice young man what the next Synergy skill is all about."

Karen blushed at that and, after a cough or two, started in. "Well, after identify strengths, align interests and positive attitude, the next skill is *don't criticize or complain.*"

"That's right," replied Tim, knowing he had taught her a lesson. "Never criticize people or complain about things. The experts feel quite strongly about this."

"Criticizing and complaining get you nothing but a tarnished reputation," Tim said. "If you have concerns, then express them in the form of questions, or suggestions. In fact, the experts teach us that questions are an excellent way of broaching touchy subjects."

Karen smiled, knowing that Tim was now playing with her. Karen, it turns out, had led the winning sales team for the prior two years, before Bob beat her last year.

"In addition," Tim continued, "you must realize that in a group setting there will always be issues, no matter what you do. Some people are going to be better than others, some more experienced. Groups are diverse, and once you accept that you will begin to expect problems rather than be surprised by them, and you'll deal with them better."

"In addition," Karen jumped in, looking for redemption, "you should always go out of your way to help people who have erred. You should try to *help them save face.*"

This time the joke was on Tim, and he took it in stride. "That's right," said Tim, "and that's yet another Synergy skill. The experts teach us that helping people to save face, to avoid embarrassment in front of others, is an invaluable skill, one that gets paid back in spades. Always remember how important people's egos are. Helping them save face is an ego saver, and they will be eternally grateful."

"I saw my uncle Prius do that just this morning. He let a business colleague named George change his contract because the deal was going to embarrass George in front of his family. Prius thought it better to let George save face by renegotiating the contract – costing him a bit in the near term but building a great relationship with George for the future."

"And I'm sure your uncle Prius will profit from his relationship with George for many years to come!" Tim said. "It's an honorable man or woman who allows someone to save face, to let them off the hook, and it's a skill that's particularly appealing to nice people."

"And someday you might find that it's you being let off the hook!" said Karen. "You will invariably end up on teams where you're not the most talented person in the group and where you make a mistake that could be costly to your reputation or career. When that happens, and when they let you save face, you should thank them and praise them for helping you."

"In fact," said Tim, "you should *praise people as often as you can, whenever you catch them doing something right.* That's the next skill of Synergy, and it's also a well-founded piece of expert advice. When you catch people doing something right and praise them for it, you boost their confidence, you encourage them to repeat what they did right, and you oil the team machine for everyone."

Bob broke in, adding: "Praising people is a nice thing to do, it's the right thing to do, and it's the way you succeed."

Tim smiled at Bob and said, "And that applies to all three Strategies for Success. *They are the nice thing to do, the right thing to do, and the way to succeed. That's why Be Nice and Win works so well for honest, caring and conscientious people – for nice people.*"

"And if you do get praised," Karen continued, "then you should go out of your way to *share the credit* – another Synergy skill. Let your boss, your customer or whomever know when other people helped you do the good work. The other people will greatly appreciate the recognition, and they'll work harder knowing that you are quick to credit their efforts. That leads to better teamwork and more success."

"Again," said Bob, "it's the nice thing to do, the right thing to do, and the way you succeed. Too many people think that sharing credit downplays their own recognition. To the contrary, most bosses are quick to recognize your self-confidence and maturity when you share credit with others, and the people you share credit with become very grateful – and better team players as a result."

"That's very true, and as a boss I should know!" said Tim, the sales director.

"And there's one more important point that I want to make," Tim continued. "People often feel that they're giving up control over their success when they work with a team – that their success will be more dependent on the team's efforts than their own. That's why *it's so important to execute the skills that are within your control* – like keeping a positive attitude, sharing credit, praising others and not criticizing them, and helping them to save face."

"For optimal Synergy," Karen said, "you need to do what's in your control to make the team work, and to make it work for you. If all team members do so, you'll get the very best Synergy!"

"And with that," Tim continued, "you now have all of the *Be Nice and Win* skills for Synergy."

The Nice Man took a deep breath, trying to digest Synergy and its skills. The sales teams were certainly well-versed in Synergy.

The Nice Man was beginning to see how everything in *Be Nice and Win* was interconnected, how it all synched.

Tim thanked the sales teams for helping teach the Nice Man about Synergy and told them to continue their group meetings until he returned. He then led the Nice Man out into the hallway.

"What do you think about my sales teams?" asked Tim.

"Well," replied the Nice Man, "they certainly know Synergy! Everything happened so quickly."

"Yes, but it's all quite easy and you'll master it in no time. Remember, *Be Nice and Win* stresses high-road skills that work with your natural character and build on your strengths as a nice person, skills that will come naturally to you and that you'll enjoy using. There's nothing in *Be Nice and Win* you can't do once you commit yourself to doing it."

*The three Strategies for Success are
the nice thing to do,
the right thing to do,
and the way to succeed.*

*That's why Be Nice and Win
works so well for honest, caring and
conscientious people – for nice people.*

SYNERGY

Recognize strengths and assign work accordingly

Align interests

Keep a positive attitude

Don't criticize or complain

Let people save face

Praise people

Share credit

"So," Tim continued, "you've now learned about Empathy and Synergy, two easy and effective Strategies for Success that guide you in your people skills and in your teamwork skills – two strategies that you can easily remember and effectively use at work to achieve success."

"And two strategies rooted in being nice," reminded the Nice Man.

"Indeed, and that's why we call it *Be Nice and Win*," Tim said. "Now, there's one sales team that was not in there that I would like you to meet. It's a very special sales team, and right now," he said, looking at his watch, "they should be in Conference Room B."

"How do you know that?" asked the Nice Man, "and why aren't they in with the other sales teams?"

"I know they're in there because that's the way they work," Tim said with a smile, "and they work on their own because they are my 'A' team – my very best sales team. They handle special projects that Prius and I assign to them."

"They sound really good," said the Nice Man. "I gather they are tops at *Be Nice and Win*?"

"Better than I, my friend," Tim replied. "Better than anyone at Prius Smith & Co., except of course for Prius himself."

Tim walked across the hall and knocked on a closed door. A voice from inside invited them in. Tim and the Nice Man went into the conference room, where two women and a man were seated around a small table. This was the "A" team, and Tim introduced them to the Nice Man.

"Doing your triage?" asked Tim.

"Better believe it," replied one of the women, whose name was Barbara.

"Well, this nice man here is learning about *Be Nice and Win*," Tim said. "He's already learned about Empathy and Synergy, and now he's ready to learn about the third and final Strategy for Success – SECURITY."

"That's great," said Barbara. "I remember first learning about *Be Nice and Win* from Prius himself when I joined the company 12 years ago. What an eye-opener!"

"For me, too," said the man, whose name was Bob. "Once I really understood that business is all about people and that I could hone my people and teamwork skills so easily, my career just took off. And I'm not even in sales!"

"You're on a sales team but not in sales?" asked the Nice Man.

"That's right," Bob said. "I'm in charge of all office and administrative work for this sales team. I keep things running smoothly here at home while Barbara and Jill hit the road selling. They love to sell, and they're great at it! And I love to keep things organized and running smoothly. We're all doing the work that we do best."

"So how do your people skills and teamwork skills help you if you're not selling?" asked the Nice Man.

"Tons!" replied Bob. "You have no idea how many people I work with every day – Legal, Human Resources, Accounting and senior management, not to mention follow-up calls I make for Barbara and Jill. I'm constantly telling myself to *Be Nice and Win* and to use my skills at Empathy, Synergy and Security to keep our sales process moving along."

Barbara spoke up, saying, "I tell myself to *Be Nice and Win* before every sales meeting. I then make sure to repeat it at least once during the meeting. It's a mental anchor for me, and the Empathy, Synergy and Security skills then come naturally."

"*Be Nice and Win* taught us all to systemize our work," Jill added, "and one of our systems is to regularly remind ourselves to *Be Nice and Win*, to use our skills in Empathy, Synergy and Security as we work."

Bob then added: "As a reminder, I keep a plaque on my desk that says '*Be Nice and Win*' on the top line and 'Empathy, Synergy and Security' on the bottom line. That way I have it in front of me all day long!"

"That's a great idea," said the Nice Man. "Can I get a plaque like that?"

"Sure," Tim replied. "We give them out to all of our employees. I'll have one waiting for you at the end of the day."

"Anyway," Tim continued, speaking to the "A" team, "do you guys want to take over for me and teach this nice young man all about Security?"

"We'd love to," Jill replied, "but in this morning's triage we had to reschedule all our projects to make time for the Markel Apparel sale that Prius asked us to finish up before tomorrow. We're going to be here all day working on it. We'd be happy to instruct him on Security – if you want to talk with Prius about extending the Markel deadline."

"No, that's okay," Tim said with a chuckle, as if there were some inside humor. "You stay focused on closing Markel and I'll continue with his initiation into *Be Nice and Win*."

"By the way," Jill said, "I have a reminder in my organizer to give you an update today on the Jones Construction sale. It's been three weeks since our presentation and the feedback has not been great. In fact, we think we might be losing the sale. I guess we were wrong to take it on – we should have let a sales team with construction industry experience handle it. Barbara and I just don't know how to sell them, and we need your help to bring them back to the table."

The Nice Man was taken aback by this frank statement of failure. This was supposed to be the "A" team. What kind of "A" team were they if their project was falling apart, they were admitting their inability to sell, and they were asking their boss to bail them out?

"Not to worry," said Tim. "I had a feeling that you might have bitten off more than you could chew. So when you took it on I made a backup plan – I told Old Man Jones that if the salespeople couldn't come to terms, I'd take him out to lunch and hammer out the deal directly between us. I'll call him this afternoon." Tim then made a note in his own organizer to do so.

"Oh, Tim, you're the best," exclaimed Jill as she gave him a big hug. "You always know what to do."

"That's because I practice *Be Nice and Win*," Tim replied, and he and the "A" team all laughed. The Nice Man knew there were some inside jokes going on, and guessed that they had something to do with the third strategy for success – Security.

So Tim and the Nice Man said their goodbyes to the "A" team, left them to work on the Markel sale, and ducked into a smaller conference room down the hall.

"Well," said Tim, "this is going to be easier than I thought."

"Why's that?" asked the Nice Man.

"Because you just saw all six Security skills in use during that conversation with my 'A' team."

"In that little chat?" replied the Nice Man. "Well then, you're going to have to explain them to me."

Tim laughed. "Before I explain the skills to you, let me tell you a little about Security, because this third *Be Nice and Win* Strategy for Success is a bit different from the first two."

"How so?" asked the Nice Man.

"Empathy and Synergy are both positive things you do with people, one-to-one people skills in the case of Empathy and teamwork skills in the case of Synergy. Security is different. *It's about protecting you − protecting your time, your energy and your work − from the many dangers in business, dangers that keep you from success.*"

"What kind of dangers?" asked the Nice Man.

"Bad dangers," Tim cautioned. "Dangers that often blindside you, take you by surprise. Dangers that will suck you in like quicksand − getting harder and harder to escape the farther in you get. Dangers that will surely keep you from success if you don't work to avoid them. And, unfortunately, dangers to which nice people like you and I are particularly vulnerable."

"Why is that?" asked the Nice Man.

"Simply a result of our being nice people in a not-so-nice, highly competitive business world. It's the nature of the beast."

"So, Empathy and Synergy are positive strategies and Security is a protective strategy. Yet, all three working together help you to act, react, and interact with people in the best way possible to hone your skills and help you succeed in business."

STRATEGY FOR SUCCESS #3

SECURITY

Security is different. It's about protecting you – protecting your time, your energy and your work – from the many dangers in business, dangers that keep you from success.

Tim smiled and nodded, proud that the Nice Man was such a quick study.

"Okay, so what are these dangers and how can I protect myself from them?" asked the Nice Man.

"Well, one of the most pernicious dangers is the weakness nice people have of saying 'yes' when they really should say 'no.' We would be much better businesspeople if we could learn to *just say 'no.*'"

"You see," Tim continued, "most people – and especially nice people – are naturally inclined to say 'yes' to things. We say 'yes' because we want to be part of whatever is going on – we want to be included. We say 'yes' because we think it's rude to say 'no.' And we say 'yes' simply because it's easier than saying 'no,' avoiding a possible confrontation."

"I can vouch for that," said the Nice Man. "I hate saying 'no' to people, and as an Amiable I hate confrontation!"

"That's exactly the danger I'm talking about," said Tim. "For example, when a friend asks you to do something, like join a committee, and you know that you really don't have the time – but you say 'yes,' thinking, 'What the heck, it couldn't take that much time, the person is a friend, and I don't want to start a confrontation over a small request …'"

"And before you know it," the Nice Man picked up, nodding his head in agreement, "you're overextended. And when you're overextended you can't give the proper time and attention to all of your commitments, so your performance slacks off and your work quality suffers. And that's bad for business."

"Exactly," said Tim. "Saying 'yes' when you should say 'no' is bad time management. The experts offer a lot of great advice on time management, and cutting down on your commitments is one of the most effective."

"Okay," said the Nice Man, "I agree that it's important to manage your time and avoid overextending yourself, to take on only things to which you can give proper time and energy. But can nice people say 'no' and still be nice?"

Tim nodded and said, "The experts teach us that there are three very effective ways to say 'no,' each used depending on the situation. As you learn *Be Nice and Win* and practice these three ways of saying 'no,' you'll become so comfortable using them that saying 'no' becomes second nature. You'll instinctively slide into whichever of the three ways is best suited for the moment."

The Nice Man understood the need to say 'no' but was still troubled by what might happen. So he asked the tough question: "But what if your boss asks you to do something? You certainly can't say 'no' to your boss!"

"Not true," said Tim. "Why, you just saw my 'A' team, my very best sales team, say 'no' to me, their boss, when I asked them to teach you about Security."

The Nice Man hadn't thought of it that way, but now he realized that the "A" team had indeed said 'no' to their boss in an indirect way.

"Now wait a minute," he said. "They actually said 'yes' to you, but told you that you would have to take care of the conflict with the Markel sale."

Tim laughed. "Exactly, and that's the first way the experts teach us to say 'no,' what we refer to as the '*your-call no*.'"

"What does that mean?" asked the Nice Man.

"The 'your-call no' is a way of saying 'no' in delicate situations, where you need to tread with the utmost respect. Just look at what my 'A' team did. They threw the decision back to me, saying they would be delighted to teach you about Security if I would adjust the Markel deadline with Prius – that it was 'my call.' Now, they knew very well that I wouldn't change the Markel deadline, so by saying it was 'my call,' by tossing it back in my lap, they were actually saying 'no' but in a nice and respectful way."

"Now I understand," replied the Nice Man. "That's a nifty way of saying 'no' without getting yourself in trouble. I like that. What are the other ways of saying 'no'?"

"The second way the experts teach us is the '*absolute no*.' With this, you look the person right in the eye and without any hesitation in your voice you give a firm and absolute 'no.'"

"The 'absolute no' is used when you want to leave no doubt in the other person's mind that you mean 'no.' Any hesitation or ambivalence and the other person will have an opening to come back at you. With the 'absolute no,' you send the clear signal that the matter is closed."

"I saw Uncle Prius do that earlier today," said the Nice Man. "A man named George asked to cancel his contract with Uncle Prius, and Prius looked him in the eye and replied with an 'absolute no.'"

"Your uncle Prius is a master at Security. How did George react to that?"

"George knew not to question him. He backed off and asked Uncle Prius how he would fix their broken agreement."

"You see," said Tim, "an 'absolute no' delivered with conviction leaves no doubt, and the conversation moves on. And while it seems tough and insensitive, it's actually the nice thing to do."

"Why is that?"

"Because nice people often try to avoid confrontation by giving a hesitant 'no.' But all that does is leave the issue open and festering, and it often comes back at you and causes even more angst in the future. It's much nicer for you, and for the other person, when you state your piece and get done with it quickly."

"But there's a third way," added Tim, "a sort of compromise between the two."

The Nice Man looked up with interest. "What's the third way?"

"It's what we call the '*polite no*.'"

"How do you do that?" asked the Nice Man.

"You look them right in the eye and with a sympathetic expression tell them 'no' while offering a kind and plausible excuse. For example, 'Oh, thank you so much for thinking of me, but with all that I have on my plate right now I'd never be able to give it the time and attention it deserves.'"

"That sounds great," said the Nice Man. "I can easily use the 'polite no' to get out of things."

"Sure," said Tim, "but you'll also need to master the 'absolute no' and the 'your-call no' as well. You'll need lots of arrows in your quiver to preserve your relationships when saying 'no,' and you'll need to practice your delivery until it's done with complete comfort and confidence."

"Just like the 'A' team did with you, moving seamlessly into the 'your-call no' when you asked them to teach me about Security."

"That's right," replied Tim. "Being able to say 'no' will keep you out of all sorts of things you don't want or need, things that will tax your time and drain your energy."

The Nice Man, however, was still puzzled by the "A" team. "Okay, so your 'A' team was able to say 'no' to you. But why do you call them your 'A' team when they are clearly not that good? I mean, they flat out told you that they are losing the Jones Construction sale. And they flat out told you that it was their fault, that they didn't know how to sell to the people at Jones Construction, and that they needed you to save them. That sounds more like a 'C' team to me!"

Tim laughed and said: "Actually, that's exactly what makes them an 'A' team, and here we have another Security skill that will protect you against a whole variety of dangers. We call this skill '*Admission*.'"

"Admission?" asked the Nice Man.

"Yes," said Tim. "*Admitting when you are wrong, when you don't know, and when you need help*."

"Those are Security skills?" asked the Nice Man.

"Absolutely," said Tim. "The danger we're talking about here is mistakes. Mistakes are the enemy of all businesspeople. They're responsible for keeping too many nice people from success."

"But everyone makes mistakes, it's only human," said the Nice Man.

"That's true," replied Tim, "and as a boss, I understand that. But I look for two things in my people: what they do to avoid mistakes, and how well they handle mistakes once they occur."

"For example?"

"For example, nothing good can come from saying 'I know' when you really don't know. So when someone says 'I don't know,' it shows me that she has a good Security system in place to help her avoid costly mistakes."

"So saying 'I don't know' helps avoid the quicksand in the first place," the Nice Man noted.

"Exactly," Tim said, "and saying 'I need help' gets you out of the quicksand before you've ventured in too deep. You see, most of the mistakes people make are relatively innocuous. A simple 'I need help' will usually reverse ship and prevent really bad consequences."

"But," the Nice Man chimed in, "when people don't ask for help – that's when it gets bad!"

"Exactly!" said Tim. "And always remember that your boss and your customers would much rather you get the work done right *with* help than wrong *without* help."

"What about 'I was wrong'?" asked the Nice Man. "I still see that as an admission of failure."

"It is. When you've done something wrong, you need to own up to it and bring closure as quickly as possible. Mistakes usually come to light sooner or later, and most people will forgive you if you act quickly. As you said before, everyone makes mistakes – it's the successful people who own up to them and then work hard to make them right."

"*So 'I don't know' avoids the quicksand, 'I need help' pulls you out, and 'I was wrong' seals it off.*"

"Precisely, and you should never underestimate the importance of these three phrases," Tim said. "They'll protect your time, your reputation, your work product and your relationships – the four cornerstones of a successful businessperson."

"That's true," agreed the Nice Man. "I guess there are lots of dangers that I've never really thought about, and lots of easy ways to avoid those dangers that I don't use very well."

"And that's why *Be Nice and Win* is so great. It's an easy and effective way to succeed."

"So Security teaches us to 'just say no' in the most appropriate of the three ways, and to nip trouble in the bud by saying 'I was wrong,' 'I don't know,' and 'I need help.' Are there any other Security skills the 'A' team showed us?"

Tim smiled and said, "Yes, but it wasn't the 'A' team, it was yours truly."

"What was it?" asked the Nice Man.

"Another skill the experts teach us to avoid dangers in business is to *anticipate*. Anticipating things to come and things that can go wrong gives you a head start on prevention and resolution. It allows you to adjust your behavior, the way you act, react, and interact, before a problem arises."

"So you thought ahead and anticipated that the 'A' team might have bitten off more than they could chew by taking on the Jones Construction sale, and you prepared for possible problems by agreeing with Old Man Jones to tie up any loose ends on your own."

"Exactly," said a smiling Tim.

"Do you need any particular skills to anticipate correctly?"

"Not at all," said Tim. "Anticipating is a discipline, just like observing people while they talk – you simply need to train yourself to do it, and the rest will follow naturally. Think about what's coming up, what other people might say or do, what dangers might come into play and how you might respond under various circumstances."

"So anticipating is a way of preparing," replied the Nice Man.

"And avoiding – avoiding the many dangers in business that keep people from success," Tim replied.

"What other Security skills did the 'A' team show us?" asked the Nice Man.

"Well, remember how I knew exactly where the "A' team would be and what they would be doing?" asked Tim.

"Yes, you said you knew that because it's the way they work."

"And the way they work is to *systemize*, to do their work in a regular and recurring way that they enjoy and that gets things done for them."

"What's so protective about that?" asked the Nice Man.

"By systemizing your work – the things you do and when you do them – you implement a process of consistency that reduces the chance of mistakes, that nagging nemesis of success."

"That's a lot like my golf game," noted the Nice Man. "I'm working on consistency for my swing. My golf pro told me that the swing should be exactly the same every time, that consistency makes perfection."

Tim nodded in agreement, adding: "And it's important that you systemize your work in a way that's enjoyable for you. The more you enjoy your system, the more likely you will be to stick with it. For example, some people like to put their calendar and to-do's on a PDA, while others prefer paper. Whatever works for you, that's what you should use."

"So you don't tell them how to systemize?"

"Absolutely not. No one, not even me, their boss, tells a team how they should systemize. Each team and each person needs to figure out their own best system, the system they will enjoy most and use. We want people to work their best, and different people work their best in different ways. On a grand scale, the important thing is not when or how you do the work, but that the work gets done and gets done correctly."

"So the 'A' team's system is to meet every day at this time to go over things?"

"That's right – what we call *triage*, which is yet another Security skill. Triage is a cross between time-management skills and organizational skills. It's an easy and important exercise of looking over all of your responsibilities and figuring out how to best accomplish them."

Tim continued: "While most teams do triage first thing in the morning, the 'A' team does triage twice a day, but they are real quick about it – 15 minutes tops to make sure that nothing falls through the cracks."

"Does their morning and afternoon triage differ?"

"Sure does," replied Tim. "In the morning, the team will focus first on 'outside business' – what they need other people to do for them. They then contact the other people about what they need. That gets people working for them first thing in the morning."

"And if they did that in the afternoon," the Nice Man picked up, "they might not be able to contact the person, or the person might be involved in other things, and then the team would have to wait another day to get what they need."

"Exactly!" said Tim. "Get other people working for you first thing in the morning. And then after they review outside business, they triage their projects and to-do's. First they'll look to see if anything on their list can be divided into smaller tasks. The 'A' team is always looking to *simplify their work* by breaking large tasks down to smaller, more manageable tasks. That makes it easier and more fun to do."

"They then focus on each task's level of importance and deadline. They want to ensure that the immediate projects get done, but also that the important projects are kept up. That's why Jill had the note in her organizer to talk with me today – the Jones Construction sale is important and she needed to make sure it didn't get overlooked."

"I saw that you made a note in your organizer to call Old Man Jones. Does everyone at Prius Smith & Co. keep an organizer?"

"Indeed they do," replied Tim. "And that's part of the final skill for Security – what we call a *'clear head.'* This is one of Prius' favorite skills because it encourages people to be productive *and* creative."

"A 'clear head' means writing down everything that you have to do and everything you have to remember. It means freeing up your brain by moving its idle content to paper, allowing you to focus one hundred percent on the task at hand and also reducing the risk of forgetting, the risk of mistake."

"That seems awfully cumbersome," the Nice Man replied.

"A bit at first, but you'll develop a system that works for you, and then it becomes easy. Actually, it becomes a pleasure – working with full confidence that what has to be done will get done, that what you must remember will be remembered – all because you have it in your organizer and you systematically use your organizer."

"And when you've cleared your head of all those details, you're free to think creatively about the work at hand, thinking with a clear head," said the Nice Man.

"You develop a whole new level of mental energy that will make you more creative and productive," Tim said. "It feels so good to free up your mind and relax, and it's so easy! All you have to do is get your system down. You don't need anything more than a calendar and a to-do list. You'll do a morning triage and perhaps another one during the day or at night. Then have fun writing everything down. And every time you write something down, think about how much easier your life is without having so much on your mind! Devote your brainpower to being more creative and productive at work."

"You make it sound so easy, so successful."

"It is, really! If you stay committed to writing everything down and doing regular triage, your system will work well, your life will be much happier and you'll be more successful at work. That I can promise you!"

Tim stepped back and said: "So there you have it – the six skills we use for Security, the third and final *Be Nice and Win* Strategy for Success."

SECURITY

Just say "no"

Say "I don't know," "I need help," "I was wrong"

Anticipate

Systemize

Triage

Clear your head

The Nice Man thought about what he had learned about *Be Nice and Win's* third strategy – Security. He had never really thought much about the dangers of business, and he now understood how easily his quest for success could be derailed by his own mistakes, by taking on too many things, by taking on things he wasn't qualified to do, and by letting things fall through the cracks.

He now appreciated how important it is to say "no" and avoid too many responsibilities. He also appreciated how easy and effective it is to say "no" using any of the three methods.

He appreciated the importance of speaking up when he is wrong, when he doesn't know, and when he needs help.

He also appreciated the importance of anticipating, thinking ahead about what's to come, what might happen, what is expected and what might go wrong. An ounce of prevention is worth a pound of cure.

He saw how systemizing your work reduces error, and he saw how clearing your head frees your mind and allows you to be more creative and productive at work. He also saw how doing triage on your organization system ensures that the right things get done at the right times in the right way.

He also thought about how Security so nicely rounds out the *Be Nice and Win* philosophy, that business is all about people. While Empathy covers one-to-one people skills and Synergy covers teamwork skills, Security covers the back end – protecting you, your time, your energy and your relationships against business dangers, dangers to which nice people are particularly vulnerable.

Finally, he thought about how easy and effective *Be Nice and Win* is. Unlike business books that inundate him with too much advice, *Be Nice and Win* simplifies the path to success into three easy strategies – Empathy, Synergy and Security – and the experts' consensus advice on each. More so, the strategies are all high-road strategies that work with his natural character and build on his strengths as a nice person.

The Nice Man felt that he had learned so much about business in the last few hours. He was now confident that he would succeed in his work using *Be Nice and Win*, and he was excited about getting back to work. He was looking forward to proving himself.

"Uncle Prius is a smart man," the Nice Man said to Tim. "Can you take me back to his office so I can thank him for teaching me all about business, all about *Be Nice and Win*?"

So Tim and the Nice Man went back up the elevator to the executive-offices floor where the Nice Man said goodbye to Tim and walked over to Uncle Prius' office.

Nancy was at her desk. She smiled when she saw him and buzzed Uncle Prius.

"Go right in," she said.

Uncle Prius got up from behind his desk. As always, he was smiling. He strode over to the Nice Man and put his arm around him.

"So, how did your day go?" he asked. "What did you learn?"

"I learned so much about *Be Nice and Win* – so much about business!" the Nice Man responded with excitement. "First I learned about Empathy and how important my people skills are to success – how important it is to understand people for what they are, and for what they are doing."

"The people you work with can make or break you," Uncle Prius said. "The better you understand their character style and the better you understand what they're really thinking, the more successful you will be."

"And I learned about Synergy from Tim and his sales teams. I saw how important teamwork is to success – how to make the team work, and make it work for me."

Uncle Prius nodded in approval. "Reality is that we live and work in teams. Those who can make the team work will be miles ahead in their quest for success."

"And," the Nice Man continued, "I learned about Security – about protecting my time, my energy, my work and my relationships from the many dangers in business."

"Dangers to which nice people are especially vulnerable," Uncle Prius added. "A natural result of our character and the competitive business world in which we work."

"And most of all," said the Nice Man, "I understand how easy it is to *Be Nice and Win*, how easy it is to use Empathy, Synergy and Security at work and to hone my skills in each. There's absolutely nothing in these Strategies for Success that I can't do!"

"But the key is to actually *do them*," Uncle Prius said sternly. "'Empathy, Synergy and Security' is the path to success, but *consistency* in their application is what keeps you moving along that path."

"I know," the Nice Man replied. "They are all within my control, and it's up to me to use them."

"And they are all you'll need to succeed," Prius said. "There's nothing more you need to succeed than good people skills, good teamwork skills and a sharp eye for danger. Don't make your life complicated. Focus on the basics. Simplify! Hone these skills and you'll be amazed at how quickly you move along your path to success."

The Nice Man nodded in agreement.

"And as a boss," Prius continued, "I've seen the wonderful impact *Be Nice and Win* has on a business. My employees are energized because they have a time-proven path to success that they can actually use – and energized employees means less turnover and greater profits for my company!"

*As a boss, I have seen the wonderful impact Be Nice and Win
has on a business.*

My employees are energized because they have a time-proven path to success that they can actually use – and energized employees means less turnover and greater profits for my company.

"*Be Nice and Win* totally changes your perspective about work," the Nice Man said. "It causes you to rethink how you relate to people – how you work with them and how you get them to work with you."

"As we like to say," Uncle Prius added, "it's the nice thing to do, it's the right thing to do, and it's how nice people succeed. In business and in life, it's so important that we stick to what we do best, and how we best do it."

Just then there was a knock at the door and Nancy came in. She went over to the Nice Man and handed him a desk plaque. The plaque read:

BE NICE and WIN
EMPATHY SYNERGY SECURITY

The Nice Man got the plaque he had asked for.

Prius sat the Nice Man down in a chair and looked him hard in the eye. "My boy, now it's up to you to *Be Nice and Win*. No one is going to do it for you. You have to take charge of your work, your attitude, your people skills and teamwork skills. You have to make it happen."

*In business and in life,
it's so important that we
stick to what we do best,
and how we best do it.*

The Nice Man understood. He was absolutely certain that he would succeed with *Be Nice and Win* and he was raring to start.

"I know, Uncle Prius," he said, "and I'm looking forward to using *Be Nice and Win* to hone my people skills and my teamwork skills, and to protect myself against mistakes and other dangers. It's my bed that I make, and if I really want to make more money, to get better work and to have more fun, then the responsibility is mine and mine alone."

"And part of that responsibility is to share *Be Nice and Win* with others, because *Be Nice and Win* is a two-way street: the better people Empathize with you – truly understand you – the better off *you* will be."

"Likewise," the Nice Man smiled, "the better people Synergize with me – the better they play on my team – the more successful I will be."

"Like it or not," Uncle Prius concluded, "business and life are team sports. Your success is greatly impacted by other people. Helping *them* to *Be Nice and Win* will help *you* to *Be Nice and Win*."

* * *

As the Nice Man walked home that afternoon, he thought about the incredible experience he just had. Uncle Prius gave him a whole new perspective on business, and he had been pointed down a path to success that was perfectly suited for his character and his strengths.

Business is indeed all about people, and your success is determined by how well you act, react, and interact with others.

"Empathy, Synergy and Security" are time-proven strategies – a path to success forged by the masters of business. However, it is up to you to use them, and also to share them with others so that they Empathize and Synergize with you.

The Nice Man now understood that Uncle Prius was right on point when he said that being nice in business is not a liability, it is an asset.

And he now truly understood what Uncle Prius meant when he said that *his greatest asset in business is that he is nice, and his greatest achievement in business is figuring out how to* Be Nice and Win.

BE NICE and WIN™

EMPATHY

Understand Their Character
- Drivers
- Expressives
- Amiables
- Analyticals

Understand Their Message
- Collect
  - Don't plot while they speak
  - Observe the nonverbal message
  - Let them talk, encourage it
- Correct
  - Think from their perspective
- Confirm
  - Concisely paraphrase the essence of the message

SYNERGY

- Recognize strengths and assign work accordingly
- Align interests
- Keep a positive attitude
- Don't criticize or complain
- Let people save face
- Praise people
- Share credit

SECURITY

- Just say "no"
- Say "I don't know," "I need help" and "I was wrong"
- Anticipate
- Systemize
- Triage
- Clear your head

JONATHAN S. BLANK

Jonathan Blank has spent 17 years simplifying complex business topics and helping others navigate their road to success.

Jonathan earned a degree in Economics from Duke University in 1985 and a law degree from the Boston University School of Law in 1988 (Editor, *International Law Journal*). He then became a member of the New York State Bar and joined Weil, Gotshal & Manges, one of the world's largest law firms, as a corporate attorney. During his three years at the law firm he specialized in mergers and acquisitions.

In 1992, Jonathan left Weil, Gotshal & Manges and joined a private financial services firm where he became head of the Asset Management Group. In 1998, he started his own investment firm and hedge fund, both of which continue to operate profitably today.

An avid tennis player, hiker and reader, Jonathan and his wife Laurie live in Alpharetta, Georgia with their three year-old daughter Danielle, one year-old twins Carly and Harrison, and their Greater Swiss Mountain Dog Toby.